Reparations
Break the Poverty Cycle

by John Marshall
© 2024 John Marshall

This book or parts thereof may not be reproduced in any form, stored in a retrieval system or transmitted in any form by any means—electronic, mechanical, photocopy, recording or otherwise—without prior written permission of the publisher, except as provided by United States of America copyright law.

Unless otherwise indicated, all Scripture taken from the NEW AMERICAN STANDARD BIBLE®, Copyright © 1960, 1962, 1963, 1968, 1971, 1972, 1973, 1975, 1977, 1995, 2020 by The Lockman Foundation. Used by permission.

© 2024 by John Marshall All rights reserved

ISBN: 979-8-9877855-3-9

Printed in the United States of America

REPARATIONS
BREAK THE POVERTY CYCLE

Introduction 1

Chapter 1: Pursue Divine Answers, not Human Questions 9

Chapter 2: Bragging Rights 17

Chapter 3: Honoring God's Preference Brings the Blessings of Life! 25

Chapter 4: Dishonoring God's Preference Brings the Curses of Life! 31

Chapter 5: You Should Forget About Sin! 37

Chapter 6: God's Preference vs. God's Tolerance 43

Chapter 7: Reparations 51

Chapter 8: For the Record 63

INTRODUCTION

INTRODUCTION

Poverty! What is it? Poverty is a state or condition in which a person or community lacks the financial resources and other essentials for a minimum standard of living. Poverty is an individual concern as well as a broader social problem. No doubt this is the poverty that Dr. Martin Luther King spoke of when in his March on Washington speech he said, *"But 100 years later, the colored American is still not free. One hundred years later, the life of the colored American is still sadly crippled by the manacles of segregation and the chains of discrimination. One hundred years later, the colored American lives on a lonely island of poverty amid a vast ocean of material prosperity. One hundred years later, the colored American is still languishing in the corners of American society and finds himself an exile in his own land. And so we've come here today to dramatize a shameful condition. In a sense, we've come to our nation's capital to cash a check. When the architects of our great republic wrote the magnificent words of the Constitution and the Declaration of Independence, they were signing a promissory note to which every American was to fall heir. This note was a promise that all men, yes, black men as well as white men, would be guaranteed the inalienable rights of life, liberty, and the pursuit of happiness. It is obvious today that America has defaulted on this promissory note insofar as her citizens of color are concerned."* This economic poverty continues to pain far too many citizens in our society.

According to Forbes, higher levels of marriage are strongly correlated with more state GDP per capita, greater levels of upward economic mobility, lower levels of child poverty, and higher median family incomes. Thus, poverty is the result of a confluence of factors, and not determined solely by income. We should eradicate poverty that is due to income. However, there is a more malignant poverty that stems from a lack of information and/or a lack of motivation to act on the information.

Jesus seemed to have encountered a man whose family suffers from malignant poverty. Someone in the crowd asked Jesus to speak to a brother about a family inheritance dispute (Luke 12:13). Likely, greed had been the root cause of the dispute. Jesus excused himself from participating, and instead, warned them to be on guard against every form of greed (Luke 12:14-15a). In addition, He also informed them that life consisted of more than the abundance of possessions, *"But He said to them, 'Beware, and be on your guard against every form of greed; for not even when one is affluent does his life consist of his possessions'"* (Luke 12:15). He illustrated this point using the parable of the rich man whom God called a fool (Luke 12:16-21). This man had lived as if life consisted of the abundance of his possessions.

However, there is a more malignant poverty as illustrated in the Jesus's warning to the rich man. Jesus told this parable to teach that earthly wealth minus God equals eternal poverty. Fools who talk to themselves fail to realize that earthly wealth minus God equals eternal poverty. They tell themselves how much they own (Luke 12:19b) and they tell themselves how long they will own it (Luke 12:19c). Fools who fail to listen to God fail to realize that earthly wealth minus God equals eternal poverty. God tells them how little they own for even their soul is required of them (Luke 12:20) and He tells them how little time they have to own it, *"'this very night, ... as for all that you have prepared, who will own it now?'"* (Luke 12:20). When we eliminate eternal poverty—operating outside of the mind and will of God—we might very well do a better job at eliminating economic poverty.

Bankrupt instructions will lead to poverty because they have no merit and simply do not work. In the absence of quality instructions quality of life never improves. How meticulously well you follow the instructions is key to reaping great rewards. The quality of your following instructions also helps to produce the quality of life that you will enjoy.

Let your mind float back to ancient days. Imagine the pageantry parade procession for a victorious Roman army general returning home from war. First, the captured prisoners of war and the confiscated merchandise shuffled along. Second, the victorious army general rode in his chariot while a slave held a jeweled crown over his head. Third and last, the victorious army strutted along for the public to view.

God reversed that order. Instead of the defeated going first, God, the conqueror, goes first. He leads His people in triumph. Triumph describes the pageantry parade procession. God always leads His people in triumph, *"leads us in triumph in Christ"* (2 Corinthians 2:14b). He positioned Himself at the forefront of their pageantry parade procession. God leads through caring persuasion; He does not drive through coercive domination.

He was the source of their success, and because of this, He became the object of their thanksgiving: *"But thanks be to God"* (2 Corinthians 2:14a). Knowledge of God produces something of value, and in Christ are the hidden treasures of wisdom and knowledge (Colossians 2:2-3).

In the Bible, knowledge of God produced a sweet fragrance. When you spray air freshener, it produces a sweet aroma, which makes the air acceptable to breathe. God manifested the sweet aroma of the knowledge of Him through His people, *"and through us reveals the fragrance of the knowledge of Him in every place"* (2 Corinthians 2:14c). The sweet fragrance of the knowledge of God that He manifests through us, those whom He led in triumph, makes His knowledge acceptable. God wants to display the success of His people for the world to see (2 Corinthians 2:14c-15, 17, 12:19, Ephesians 3:10).

To be blessed is to be positioned for prosperity – the God-caused success in all areas of life. To be positioned for prosperity is to have people and circumstances, factors, and forces favorably synchronized on your behalf. The lame man had not been blessed with healing (John 5:1-9). When the water was moved, no one was present to put him in the water. When one was available to place him in the water, the water had not been stirred. Until Jesus came along, factors and forces had not been synchronized favorably for him because he was not positioned; therefore, he had not been blessed.

Unlike the lame man, Isaac was blessed—amid a famine—because he was favorably positioned, synchronized, and aligned Isaac with people and circumstances for prosperity for the world to see, *"Now there was a famine in the land, besides the previous famine that had occurred in the days of Abraham. So Isaac went to Gerar, to Abimelech king of the Philistines. And the Lord appeared to him and said, 'Do not go down to Egypt; stay in the land of which I shall tell you. Live for a time in this land and I will be with you and bless you, for to you and to your descendants I will give all these lands, and I will establish the oath which I swore to your father Abraham. I will multiply your descendants as the stars of heaven, and will give your descendants all these lands; and by your descendants all the nations of the earth shall be blessed'... Now Isaac sowed in that land and reaped in the same year a hundred times as much. And the Lord blessed him, and the man became rich, and continued to grow richer until he became very wealthy; for he had possessions of flocks and herds, and a great household, so that the Philistines envied him"* (Genesis 26:1-4 and 12-14).

Despite being lied on by Potiphar' wife, God blessed Joseph. God favorably positioned, synchronized, and aligned Joseph with people and circumstances for prosperity for the world to see, *"And the Lord was with Joseph, so he became a successful man. And he was in the house of his master, the Egyptian. Now his master saw that the Lord was with him and that the Lord made all that he did prosper in his hand. So Joseph found favor in his sight and became his personal servant; and he made him overseer over his house, and put him in charge of all that he owned. It came about that from the time he made him overseer in his house and over all that he owned, the Lord blessed the Egyptian's house on account of Joseph; so the Lord's blessing was upon all that he owned, in the house and in the field"* (Genesis 39:2-5).

Despite extreme losses, God blessed Job. God favorably positioned, synchronized, and aligned Job with people and circumstances for prosperity for the world to see, *There was a man in the land of Uz whose name was Job; and that man was blameless, upright, fearing God and turning away from evil. Seven sons and three daughters were born to him. His possessions were seven thousand sheep, three thousand camels, five hundred yoke of oxen, five hundred female donkeys, and very many servants; and that man was the greatest of all the men of the east Now there was a day when the sons of God came to present themselves before the Lord, and Satan also came among them. The Lord said to Satan, 'From where do you come?' Satan answered the Lord and said, 'From roaming about on the earth and walking around on it.' The Lord said to Satan, 'Have you considered My servant Job? For there is no one like him on the earth, a blameless and upright man, fearing God and turning away from evil.' Then Satan answered the Lord, 'Does Job fear God for nothing?* [10] *Have You not made a fence around him and his house and all that he has, on every side? You have blessed the work of his hands, and his possessions have increased in the land'"* (Job 1:1-10).

In this book, we will uncover God's principles as it relates to breaking the poverty cycle in the following sections:

We must Pursue Divine Answers, not Human Questions, which entails the pursuit of divine answers and not human questions. We must operate with the mind of Christ to for successful life navigation.

Bragging Rights permits us to highly esteem our spiritual connection by boasting in the Lord, which minimizes our our human accomplishment in favor of maximizing our accomplishment in Christ.

Honoring God's Preference Brings the Blessings of Life, which is a blueprint for blessings. Deuteronomy 28 clearly outlines that there are blessings for obedience.

Conversely, **Dishonoring God's Preference Brings the Curses of Life**. To experience the blessings of God to their fullest extent, we cannot dishonor God's commands. To be carnally minded is death, but to be spiritually minded is life and peace; therefore, **You Should Forget About Sin** and instead remember God's preferences for Christian conduct.

God's Preference vs. God's Tolerance outlines God's perfect versus permissive will. To succeed in Christ, we must know the difference.

And finally, **Reparations**. While reparations are often associated with monetary or material gain, the Bible emphasizes *mental* versus *metal* reparations, where our minds are renewed as we are transformed to live a new life according to the will of God.

CHAPTER ONE

PURSUE DIVINE ANSWERS, NOT HUMAN QUESTIONS

PURSUE DIVINE ANSWERS, NOT HUMAN QUESTIONS

Why is there so much division in church (religious) teachings? And how do we fix it?

If you want to know what my thoughts are about anger management, you must consult with me. Fortunately for you, I have written my thoughts in my book *Good and Angry*. When you read my book, you can know my thoughts on the matter of anger management.

If you want to know which tax deductions are allowed by the IRS, you must consult with the IRS. Fortunately for you, the IRS has written their guidelines in the Internal Revenue Tax code. When you read the Internal Revenue Tax Code, you can know the IRS's guidelines regarding tax deductions.

If you want to know what God's thoughts are about any subject, you must consult with Him. Fortunately for us, God has deposited His thoughts in the book, the Bible. When we read His book, the Bible, we can know His thoughts on the subject, *"as I wrote before briefly. By referring to this, when you read you can understand my insight into the mystery of Christ"* (Ephesians 3:3-4).

Please internalize and realize these pertinent truths. The mind of God (scripture) holds the answers, while the human mind hosts the questions. Therefore, when we delve into the mind of God, we discover answers, but when we delve into the human mind, we only discover questions.

Where should we begin our search for truth? Where do we start our investigation for truth? Far too often, we err into divisiveness because we begin our search with our questions rather than His answers.

Illustrations: The religious people of Jesus' day just never seemed to be able to understand accurately. Though wisdom had taught them, they seemed to have never been able to come to the full knowledge of truth (2 Timothy 3:6). Why?

"On that day some Sadducees (who say there is no resurrection) came to Jesus and questioned Him, saying, 'Teacher,' Moses said, 'If a man dies having no children, his brother as next of kin shall marry his wife, and raise up children for his brother.' Now there were seven brothers among us; and the first married and died, and having no children, he left his wife to his brother. It was the same also with the second brother, and the third, down to the seventh. Last of all, the woman died. In the resurrection, therefore, whose wife of the seven will she be? For they all had her in marriage.'

But Jesus answered and said to them, 'You are mistaken, since you do not understand the Scriptures nor the power of God'" (Matthew 22:23-29).

They started their search with an investigation question (Matthew 22:23-28). Their investigation question led them to focus on how circumstances applied to others. This resulted in nothing more than inaction of distraction on the part of the questioner.
They should have started their search with an application answer (Matthew 22:29). An application answer would have led them to focus on how scripture applied to themselves. This would have resulted in an action of satisfaction.

"And it happened that He was passing through the grainfields on the Sabbath, and His disciples began to make their way along while picking the heads of grain. The Pharisees were saying to Him, 'Look, why are they doing what is not lawful on the Sabbath?' And He said to them, 'Have you never read what David did when he was in need and he and his companions became hungry'" (Mark 2:23-25).

They started their search with an investigation question (Mark 2:23-24). Their investigation question led them to focus on how circumstances applied to others. This resulted in nothing more than inaction of distraction.

They should have started their search with an application answer (Mark 2:25-28, 1 Samuel 21:1-6). An application answer would have led them to focus on how scripture applied to themselves. This would have resulted in an action of satisfaction.

"The Pharisees and some of the scribes gathered to Him after they came from Jerusalem, and saw that some of His disciples were eating their bread with unholy hands, that is, unwashed. (For the Pharisees and all the other Jews do not eat unless they carefully wash their hands, thereby holding firmly to the tradition of the elders; and when they come from the marketplace, they do not eat unless they completely cleanse themselves; and there are many other things which they have received as traditions to firmly hold, such as the washing of cups, pitchers, and copper pots) And the Pharisees and the scribes asked Him, 'Why do Your disciples not walk in accordance with the tradition of the elders, but eat their bread with unholy hands?' But He said to them, 'Rightly did Isaiah prophesy about you hypocrites, as it is written: "This people honors Me with their lips, But their heart is far away from Me. ⁷And in vain do they worship Me, Teaching as doctrines the commandments of men." Neglecting the commandment of God, you hold to the tradition of men.' He was also saying to them, 'You are experts at setting aside the commandment of God in order to keep your tradition'" (Mark 7:1-9).

They started their search with an investigation question (Mark 7:1-5). Their investigation question led them to focus on how circumstances applied to others. This resulted in nothing more than inaction of distraction. They should have started their search with an application answer (Mark 7:6-9). An application answer would have led them to focus on how scripture applied to themselves. This would have resulted in an action of satisfaction.

"And He said to them, 'Go into all the world and preach the gospel to all creation. The one who has believed and has been baptized will be saved; but the one who has not believed will be condemned'" (Mark 16:15-16).

People start their search with an investigation question. Their investigation question leads them to focus on how circumstances apply to others. Here are some invalid questions they ask that leads to nothing more than the inaction of distraction:

What about a person who dies on the way to get baptized?
What about a person in a third-world country who has never heard about baptism?
What about people who have been baptized but are not living right?
What about the thief on the cross?
What's in the water?
What if there is no water nearby?

They should start their search with an application answer (Mark 16:16). An application answer would lead them to focus on how scripture applies to them. This would result in an action of satisfaction (Acts 2:38, 1 Peter 3:21).

Recommendations:

1. Start with the answers. Do not start with the questions.
2. Start with answers from the mind of God. Do not start with questions from within the human mind.
3. Start with the answers from within scripture. Do not start with questions from within human experiences and circumstances.
4. Carve out answers from the adequately informed mind of God. Do not create questions from the inadequately informed human mind.
5. Seek to honor principles from scripture. Do not see to harmonize people of the circumstances.
6. Out of your mind, do seek to express divine answers from within scripture. Do not, out of your mind, seek to extract human questions from within circumstances.

Please internalize and realize these pertinent truths. The mind of God (scripture) holds the answers, while the human mind hosts the questions. Therefore, when we delve into the mind of God, we discover answers, but when we delve into the human mind, we only discover questions.

Am I spending time pursuing an application answer, or am I just spending time pursuing an investigation question that applies to something else?

CHAPTER TWO

BRAGGING RIGHTS

BRAGGING RIGHTS

Position and Power

When was the last time that you complimented your accomplishments? When was the last time you overstated your accomplishments? When was the last time you bragged about yourself?

What did you boast about? Did you brag about your position? Or did you brag about your power?

Little children will accomplish something and then say, "Look at me!" Adults will accomplish something and then say, "Look at me!" While we were in the womb God embedded a "bragging gene" that lasts until we are in the tomb.

God knew that we needed something to brag about. Therefore, He authorized His people to boast. He replaced their unhealthy basis with His healthy basis for boasting.

In the culture of that day, death on a cross was foolish, weak, and despised (Mark 15:27-32, Luke 24:13-21). However, Jesus' death on the cross proved to be wise, mighty, and noble. Nothing had (and nothing ever will) ever been more significant than the crucifixion, death, burial, and resurrection of Jesus, for it instituted the system of Christianity.

Through the preaching of the cross, God established His superiority. We ought to weave the message of the cross into our everyday thinking. What actually is the message of the cross?

The message of the cross is about position, a fundamental human boasting entity. For those who would believe, the message of the cross positioned them into Christ to be saved by God, saved from the penalty, power and presence of sin (1 Corinthians 1:18, 21, Acts 18:1-8). To those who refused to believe, that same message was foolishness (1 Corinthians 1:18, 20, 22-23, 25).

The message of the cross is about power, a fundamental human boasting entity. For those who would believe, the message of the cross powered them to be wise, strong, and noble. To those who refused to believe, that same message was ignorant, weak, and despised (1 Corinthians 1:26-28).

No one had ever been wise enough to design a system that eradicated evil in the world. Some had created ethical and moral systems, but no one had ever been able to honor the very system they created. Through Jesus, God created a system and provided the power for His people to be righteous, sanctified and redeemed (1 Corinthians 1:30-31).

Observations:

1. The cross eliminates boasting before God (1 Corinthians 1:29, 3:21).

2. The cross perpetuates boasting in God (1 Corinthians 1:31, 4:7, Jeremiah 9:23).

God wants you to champion His wisdom as the ultimate instructor of human thought and behavior. His wisdom centers on the preaching of the cross. God demonstrated His superiority. He used what they believed to be foolish and demonstrated it to be wise and used what they believed to be weak and demonstrated it to be strong.

In other words, the least "whatever" of God was superior to the greatest "whatever" of man (1 Corinthians 1:18-25). Illustration: Compare me to the Hall of Fame baseball player Jim Rice, who by the way is a native of Anderson, SC. His worst day at bat would be better than my best day at bat and his worse day in the field would be better than my best day in the field. He used that which was considered foolish and used that which was *not* significant. He used that which was not significant in the human mind to shame = humiliate (1 Corinthians 11:4-5, 22), nullify = render powerless (1 Corinthians 2:6, 6:13, 13:8, 10-11, 15:24) to reduce that which was significant in the human mind.

Human Eloquence or Divine Education

Throughout the letter, the Apostle Paul sprinkled this letter with negative prohibitions. To the negative, he attached positive solicitations. On that couplet, he sprinkled "so that" sauce (1 Corinthians 1:14-15, 16-17, 27-31, 2:5, 12, 3:18, 4:6, 8).

The message of the cross was the Death Burial and Resurrection of Jesus. The message of Death, Burial, and Resurrection ushered in the system of Christianity. The message of the cross, the Death Burial and Resurrection of Jesus exceeded the intellectual capacity of the unaided human mind (1 Corinthians 2:14).

The message of the cross was not revealed from the human spirit (1 Corinthians 2:9). Instead, the message of the cross was revealed by the Holy Spirit (1 Corinthians 2:10-16). The Holy Spirit revealed the very words of God (1 Corinthians 2:13).

A negative prohibition exists in the first couplet (1 Corinthians 2:1-4a). And there exists a positive solicitation (1 Corinthians 2:4b). They couple together to form a "so that" (1 Corinthians 2:5-9).

A negative prohibition exists in the second couplet (1 Corinthians 2:10-12a). And there exists a positive solicitation (1 Corinthians 2:12b). They couple together to form a "so that" (1 Corinthians 2:12c-16).

The Corinthians had become infatuated with the language of worldly wisdom. Their infatuation led them to boast in the wisdom language of their leaders (1 Corinthians 1:12, 3:21-23). This boasting had caused division within the church.

The Apostle Paul reminded them that God had eliminated human achievement as a basis for boasting (1 Corinthians 1:26-29). He pointed out and demonstrated that divine accomplishment was their only basis for boasting (1 Corinthians 1:3, 31, 4:7). Therefore, boasting in God enabled them to establish their faith in the power of God (1 Corinthians 2:5).

The Apostle Paul engaged in the effectual preaching of the cross to get them to boast in God. The negative: the effectual preaching of the cross would lead them to not rest their faith on the wisdom of men. The positive: the effectual preaching of the cross would lead them to rest their faith on the power of God.

In Athens, the Apostle Paul deliberately avoided the advantages of human eloquence. He showered his audience with the profoundness of human wisdom, beginning his speech with his knowledge of them and ending it with the resurrection of Jesus (Acts 17:16-31). Despite the brilliance of his speech, he converted only a few (Acts 17:32-34). In Corinth, the Apostle Paul deliberately avowed the advantages of divine education. He showered his audience with the profoundness of divine wisdom. He began his speech with his knowledge of Christ and Him crucified and ended his speech with the knowledge of Christ and Him crucified (1 Corinthians 2:1-2). In spite of the simplicity of his speech, he converted many (Acts 18: 4-8). He taught both audiences to build their faith in the resurrection and to build up their faith on the resurrection.

Stark Contrast: Human Eloquence vs Divine Education

The Apostle Paul contrasted human eloquence with divine education. They had elevated human eloquence at the expense of divine education. Divine education proved to be far more valuable.

Human eloquence led them remain fleshly, immature and in need of milk. Divine education would have led them to be spiritual, mature, and able to consume meat (1 Corinthians 3:3a). He had hoped to give them meat, but he had had to give them milk.
Human eloquence led them destructively into jealousy and strife (1 Corinthians 3:3b). Divine education led them constructively into planting and building (1 Corinthians 3:9

Human eloquence had led them to forget that they were just workers. Divine education would have led them to remember that they were just workers (1 Corinthians 3:1-5).

Human eloquence led them to maximize the human and minimize the divine factor. Divine education would have led them to minimize the human and maximize the divine (1 Corinthians 3:6-8). Paul had corrected their sinful view and given them a scriptural view.

CHAPTER THREE

HONORING GOD'S PREFERENCE BRINGS THE BLESSINGS OF LIFE!

HONORING GOD'S PREFERENCE BRINGS THE BLESSINGS OF LIFE!

"See, I am placing before you today a blessing and a curse: the blessing, if you listen to the commandments of the Lord your God, which I am commanding you today" (Deuteronomy 11:26-27).

God often led His people by caring persuasion, not coercive domination. He left room for them to rebel. Our Lord wanted to protect His people, but they were unwilling, and He did not force them. *Jerusalem, Jerusalem, the city that kills the prophets and stones those who have been sent to her! How often I wanted to gather your children together, just as a hen gathers her young under her wings, and you were unwilling!* (Luke 13:34). God set the blessing of life before the Hebrews. Time and time again, they rejected life.

Those to whom He spoke had witnessed the power and blessings of God, *"Know this day that I am not speaking with your sons who have not known and who have not seen the discipline of the Lord your God ... but your own eyes have seen all the great work of the Lord which He did"* (Deuteronomy 11:2-7). Therefore, He reminded them of the protective provisions of God, *"His greatness, His mighty hand, His outstretched arm, and His signs and His works which He did in the midst of Egypt to Pharaoh the king of Egypt and to all his land; and what He did to Egypt's army, to its horses and its chariots, when He made the water of the Red Sea engulf them while they were pursuing you, and the Lord completely eliminated them; and what He did to you in the wilderness, until you came to this place"* (Deuteronomy 11:2b-5).

Earlier in this discourse, God expressed His behavior preference, *"You shall therefore love the Lord your God, and always keep His directive, His statutes, His ordinances, and His commandments"* (Deuteronomy 11:1). He promised the blessings of life to those who honored His behavior preference, *"You shall therefore keep every commandment which I am commanding you today, so that you may be strong and go in and take possession of the land into which you are about to cross to possess it; and so that you may prolong your days on the land which the Lord swore to your fathers to give to them and to their descendants, a land flowing with milk and honey"* (Deuteronomy 11:8, 9). Did you notice the *"so thats"*?

Even now, God expresses His behavior preference for His kingdom citizens. He promises the blessings of life to those who honor His preference. God's blessings may be tangible and visible or intangible and invisible. But whether you notice God's blessings or not, God always rewards us for honoring His preference, *"But, beloved, we are convinced of better things regarding you, and things that accompany salvation, even though we are speaking in this way. For God is not unjust so as to forget your work and the love which you have shown toward His name, by having served and by still serving the saints"* (Hebrews 6:9-10). You win when you stay in His preference (Matthew 6:33, Luke 18:28-30, John 12:26, 1 Samuel 2:30).

When we honor God's preference, He blesses us with a better quality of life, *"And now, Israel, what does the Lord your God require of you, but to fear the Lord your*

God, to walk in all His ways and love Him, and to serve the Lord your God with all your heart and with all your soul, and to keep the Lord's commandments and His statutes which I am commanding you today for your good?" (Deuteronomy 10:12-13). Honoring God's preference was for their good. Additional scriptures testify that honoring God's preference improves the quality of life (Deuteronomy 11:8, 13-15, 22-25).

When we honor God's preference, He blesses us with a better quantity of life, *"You shall therefore keep every commandment which I am commanding you today, so that you may be strong and go in and take possession of the land into which you are about to cross to possess it; and so that you may prolong your days on the land which the Lord swore to your fathers to give to them and to their descendants, a land flowing with milk and honey"* (Deuteronomy 11:8-9). Honoring God's preference was good for them. Additional scriptures testify that honoring God's preference increases the quantity of life (Deuteronomy 11:19-21, Exodus 20:12, Ephesians 6:2).

Are you desiring God's preference reward while engaging in tolerance habits? God wants you to follow each divine instruction meticulously.

Behavior should no longer be a right and wrong issue. Immature believers still ask, "Is it right or is it wrong"? Mature believers only ask, "Does it honor God's preference?" Does it honor God's preference for believers to study the Bible individually and collectively and worship him individually and collectively?

In an upcoming article, we will discover how to determine God's preference.

CHAPTER FOUR

DISHONORING GOD'S PREFERENCE BRINGS THE CURSES OF LIFE!

DISHONORING GOD'S PREFERENCE BRINGS THE CURSES OF LIFE!

"But it shall come about, if you do not obey the Lord your God, to be careful to follow all His commandments and His statutes which I am commanding you today, that all these curses will come upon you and overtake you: Cursed will you be in the city, and cursed will you be in the country. Cursed will be your basket and your kneading bowl. Cursed will be the children of your womb, the produce of your ground, the newborn of your herd, and the offspring of your flock. Cursed will you be when you come in, and cursed will you be when you go out" (Deuteronomy 28:15-19).

In the beginning, God set two options before Adam and Eve: the blessing of life and the curse of death, *"The Lord God commanded the man, saying, 'From any tree of the garden you may freely eat; but from the tree of the knowledge of good and evil you shall not eat, for on the day that you eat from it you will certainly die'"* (Genesis 2:16-17). Through *"any tree of the garden,"* God provided all that they needed to sustain life vibrantly. He set a prohibition on a single tree; the tree of the knowledge of good and evil. However, they still chose the curse of disobedience, *"When the woman saw that the tree was good for food, and that it was a delight to the eyes, and that the tree was desirable to make one wise, she took some of its fruit and ate; and she also gave some to her husband with her, and he ate"* (Genesis 3:6). Unfortunately, they chose the curse of death.

For the Hebrews, God expressed His behavior preference, *"You shall therefore love the Lord your God, and always keep His directive, His statutes, His ordinances, and His commandments"* (Deuteronomy 11:1). He then allowed them to choose the blessing of life or the curse of death, *"See, I am placing before you today a blessing and a curse: the blessing, if you listen to the commandments of the Lord your God, which I am commanding you today; and the curse, if you do not listen to the commandments of the Lord your God, but turn aside from the way which I am commanding you today, by following other gods which you have not known"* (Deuteronomy 11:26-28). But just as Adam had done earlier, they chose the curse.

Why? Was it through ignorance? No! They had witnessed His power and blessings (Deuteronomy 11:2-7). They were aware of His protective provisions, for He had displayed and demonstrated His power on their behalf on numerous occasions. But it was all to no avail.

When they dishonored God's preference, He cursed them with a lesser quality of life – they lived poorer, *"Beware that your hearts are not easily deceived, and that you do not turn away and serve other gods, and worship them. Otherwise, the anger of the Lord will be kindled against you, and He will shut up the sky so that there will be no rain, and the ground will not yield its produce; then you will quickly perish from the good land which the Lord is giving you"* (Deuteronomy 11:16-17). Because they failed to honor God's preference, they experienced famine after famine and frustration after frustration.

When they dishonored God's preference, He cursed them with a lesser quantity of life – they died sooner, *"The Lord will send against you curses, panic, and rebuke, in everything you undertake to do, until you are destroyed and until you perish quickly, on account of the evil of your deeds, because you have abandoned Me. The Lord will make the plague cling to you until He has eliminated you from the land where you are entering to take possession of it. The Lord will strike you with consumption, inflammation, fever, feverish heat, and with the sword, with blight, and with mildew, and they will pursue you until you perish. The heaven which is over your head shall be bronze, and the earth which is under you, iron. The Lord will make the rain of your land powder and dust; from heaven it shall come down on you until you are destroyed. The Lord will cause you to be defeated by your enemies; you will go out one way against them, but you will flee seven ways from their presence, and you will be an example of terror to all the kingdoms of the earth. Your dead bodies will serve as food for all birds of the sky and for the animals of the earth, and there will be no one to frighten them away"* (Deuteronomy 28:20-26). They caused their own pain.

Even now, for His kingdom citizens, God expresses His behavior preference (1 Peter 3:7-9). He disciplines and withholds favor from those who dishonor His expressed preference (Hebrews 12:11, 1 Peter 3:10-12). Whether you notice it or not, God penalizes you for dishonoring His preference. Whenever you are out of His preference, you lose. Therefore, you would be wise not to proceed to do that which He has not expressed prohibition but proceed to do that which He has expressed preference.

CHAPTER FIVE

YOU SHOULD FORGET ABOUT SIN!

YOU SHOULD FORGET ABOUT SIN!

After the Hebrews crossed the Red Sea and began their journey to the Promised Land, God expressed His preference for them. He preferred that the Hebrews heed His voice, do right in His sight, and keep His commandments. For their conformity to His preference, God promised to reward the Hebrews with a disease-free lifestyle, *"Then he cried out to the Lord, and the Lord showed him a tree; and he threw it into the waters, and the waters became sweet. There He made for them a statute and regulation, and there He tested them. And He said, "If you will listen carefully to the voice of the Lord your God, and do what is right in His sight, and listen to His commandments, and keep all His statutes, I will put none of the diseases on you which I have put on the Egyptians; for I, the Lord, am your healer"* (Exodus 15:25-26).

It was not His preference for them but rather His preference for Himself. He wanted to withhold all diseases from their midst. But His preference was conditional upon their behavior. In other words, if they honored His preference, He would grant blessings to them, resulting in maximum quality of life. If they dishonored His preference, He would withhold blessings from them, resulting in a less-than-maximum quality of life.

Right before He removed the seven greater and stronger nations, God expressed His preference for the Hebrews. He preferred that the Hebrews hear and obey His covenant. For their conformity to His preference, God promised to reward the Hebrews with productivity and a disease-free lifestyle, *"Then it shall come about, because you listen to these judgments and keep and do them, that the Lord your God will keep His covenant with you and His faithfulness which He swore to your forefathers. And He will love you, bless you, and make you numerous; He will also bless the fruit of your womb and the fruit of your ground, your grain, your new wine, and your oil, the newborn of your cattle and the offspring of your flock, in the land which He swore to your forefathers to give you. You shall be blessed above all peoples; there will be no sterile male or infertile female among you or among your cattle. And the Lord will remove from you all sickness; and He will not inflict upon you any of the harmful diseases of Egypt which you have known, but He will give them to all who hate you"* (Deuteronomy 7:12-15).

It was not His preference for them but rather His preference for Himself. He wanted to withhold all lack of productivity and diseases from their midst. But His preference was conditional upon their behavior. In other words, if they honored His preference, He would grant blessings to them, resulting in maximum quality of life. If they dishonored His preference, He would withhold blessings from them, resulting in a less-than-maximum quality of life.

When Joshua received His leadership coronation after Moses died, God expressed His preference for the Hebrews. He preferred that the Hebrews be robust, courageous, and precisely obedient. For their conformity to His preference, God promised to reward the Hebrews with a prosperous lifestyle, *"Only be strong and very courageous; be careful to do according to all the Law which Moses My servant commanded you; do not turn from it to the right or to the left, so that you may achieve success wherever you go. This Book of the Law shall not depart from your mouth, but you shall meditate on it day and night, so that you may be careful to do according to all that is written in it; for then you will make your way prosperous, and then you will achieve success"* (Joshua 1:7-8).

It was not His preference for them but rather His preference for Himself. He wanted to withhold all lack of prosperity from their midst. But His preference was conditional upon their behavior. In other words, if they honored His preference, He would grant blessings to them, resulting in maximum quality of life. If they dishonored His preference, He would withhold blessings from them, resulting in a less-than-maximum quality of life.

It is evident that our quality of life is better when we honor God's preference and that our quality of life deteriorates when we dishonor God's preference. Is your objective to discover what honors God's preference (righteousness) and walk towards it, or is it to discover what dishonors God's preference (sin/tolerance) and walk away from it? Make no mistake; these two are not the same. They are not even close kin. The first looks for the road and maneuvers to stay in it, while the other looks for the ditch and swerves from it.

The mature never ask, "Is it sin?" They only ask, "Is it God's preference?" If you are still concerned about right and wrong, I invite you to live in the "preference" suite.

CHAPTER SIX

GOD'S PREFERENCE VS. GOD'S TOLERANCE

GOD'S PREFERENCE VS. GOD'S TOLERANCE

There exists tension within the biblical text. Not only is there tension but there is so much tension that human beings will never fully resolve some teachings from within the text, "as also in all his letters, speaking in them of these things, in which there are some things that are hard to understand, which the untaught and unstable distort, as they do also the rest of the Scriptures, to their own destruction" (2 Peter 3:16). Even among scholarly students of scripture, there exists tension. Some days, I think God may have designed the word to create tension lest we believe we have mastered His wisdom. But whether the tension is incidental or intentional, He recognized it would exist.

Though each of us will stand to be judged, we are not to judge one another (Romans 14:10-13).

Some, out of good conscience, will believe that some things are unclear. In contrast, others will think they're crystal clear (Romans 14:14). At best, God either failed to place clarity within His word or we humans have been unable to develop complete comprehensibility to understand His word intelligently.

Every passage of scripture has God's authorial intent. God intended to convey a specific message. We search for His authorial intent through literal grammatical and historical analytical gymnastics.

God intentionally indicates His preference through prescriptive statements. Observe the underlined texts. *"Therefore, ridding yourselves of falsehood, speak truth each one of you with his neighbor, because we are parts of one another. Be angry, and yet do not sin; do not let the sun go down on your anger, and do not give the devil an opportunity. The one who steals must no longer steal; but rather he must labor, producing with his own hands what is good, so that he will have something to share with the one who has need. Let no unwholesome word come out of your mouth, but if there is any good word for edification according to the need of the moment, say that, so that it will give grace to those who hear. Do not grieve the Holy Spirit of God, by whom you were sealed for the day of redemption. All bitterness, wrath, anger, clamor, and slander must be removed from you, along with all malice. Be kind to one another, compassionate, forgiving each other, just as God in Christ also has forgiven you"* (Ephesians 4:25-32).

God expressed His preference, *"My little children, I am writing these things to you so that you may not sin"* (1 John 2:1a). In this instance, we can readily know God's preference for by the statement He informs us that He prefers sinless perfection. I must admit that He does not always state His preference this succinctly. In those instances, we must engage the text more deliberately.

How much does it surprise you that God prefers sinless perfection? How do you process God's preference? Does it shock you that God still prefers sinless perfection despite human frailty?

Immediately after expressing His preference, God states His tolerance, *"And if anyone sins, we have an Advocate with the Father, Jesus Christ the righteous; and He Himself is the propitiation for our sins; and not for ours only, but also for the sins of the whole world"* (1 John 2:1b-2). Yes, He tolerates less than sinless perfection of human behavior.

Some may think that sin would abound even more if God offered forgiveness, a remedy for sin. Some among the Roman disciples did believe and behave according to that thinking. However, the Apostle Paul rebuked that immature and erroneous thinking (Romans 6:1-6).

How do God's preference and His tolerance synchronize? They synchronize in Jesus. Human beings fail and will fail. Jesus succeeded. God accepts Jesus' accomplishments. His sinless perfection is the propitiation of adequate satisfaction for the world's sins. Jesus satisfied God's righteous demand for justice.

Because God leads by caring persuasion, not coercive domination, He leaves room for ignorant and intentional rebellion. God has a preference, which is His ideal will. God has a tolerance, which is less than His ideal will.

We should desire to pursue God's ideal will. We should not desire to know what is less than His ideal will. Let us never get comfortable striving only for God's tolerance instead of His preference.

Honoring God's preference improves our quality of life (Deuteronomy 11:1- 21, Joshua 1:7, Matthew 6:33, 11:28- 30, 1 Timothy 4:8). Thus, we should diligently desire to understand God's will and honor His preference.

How will we know His will? How can we know His preference? In addition to making His preference known through prescriptive and prohibitive statements, God also indicates His preference through accounts of approved actions. In chapter 25 of his gospel, Matthew recorded three of Jesus' "end-of-time" parables: the parable of the ten virgins, the parable of the talents, and the parable of the sheep and goats. The parable of the talents emphasized accountability. A talent was a piece of money that weighed approximately 200 lbs. and was equivalent to 15 years' worth of wages.

Before going on a journey, a certain lord entrusted his money to his three servants (Matthew 25:14-15). One servant received one talent (200 lbs. of gold), another servant received two talents (400 lbs. of gold), and yet another servant received five talents (1,000 lbs. of gold).

The servant who had received the five talents engaged in commerce and gained five more talents (Matthew 25:20). The servant who had received two talents engaged in commerce and gained two more talents (Matthew 25:22). Though there is no indicator that the master had told the servants what to do, his compliment and reward indicated his approval (Matthew 25:21, 23).

This account of approved action indicates God's preference. God prefers that His servants improve their abilities and engage in activities that increase their assets. Initially, the master allocated the talents according to each servant's abilities (Matthew 25:15). Obviously, their abilities increased, increasing their assets.

While passing through Samaria on His way to Jerusalem, Jesus encountered ten lepers who asked for mercy (Luke 17:11-13). We know that one was not a Jew, for he was a Samaritan. Likely, the other nine were Jews. Lepers were religiously banned from socialization and the worship of the temple. They were not allowed to live within the walls of the township.

Jesus sent the lepers to show themselves to the priest and healed them as they were going, *"When He saw them, He said to them, 'Go and show yourselves to the priests.' And as they were going, they were cleansed"* (Luke 17:14b). But why did Jesus send them to the priest? The Law of Moses, the jurisdictional law under which Jesus lived, banned lepers from the common community until after the priest had offered a sacrifice and vouched for their healing (Leviticus 14:1-32).

Even when he had no leprosy, the Samaritan was not allowed to enter the temple, so there was no need for him to show himself to the priest. Thus, he returned to Jesus, "glorifying God" with a loud voice (Luke 17:15-16), and Jesus approved (Luke 17:17-19). This account of action indicates God's preference for placing the praise of His glory as a priority in human affairs.

Some men came down from Judea and taught that *"unless you are circumcised according to the custom of Moses, you cannot be saved"* (Acts 15:1b). Paul and Barnabas vehemently opposed this teaching. Their opposition to this conflict led to a council in Jerusalem (Acts 15:24). Therein, God indicated His preference.

He approves of believers coming together to intensely discuss (debate) religious differences (Act 15:22-29). Paul, Barnabas, and others traveled to Jerusalem.

He approves of believers reaching an agreement to solve religious differences. The whole church came to an accepted conclusion (Acts 15:22).

He approves of believers solving their differences based on God's authoritative actions. They discussed the issue given what God had done (Acts 15:7-9, 10:44-48).

He approves of believers solving their differences based on the authoritative advice of the Apostles, who made recommendations that the whole church accepted (Acts 15:18- 22).

He approves of believers understanding that the resurrection of Jesus released the followers of Jesus from the binding restrictions of circumcision (Acts 15:24).

He approves of believers recommending approved courses of action to other believers (Acts 15:22-24).

He approves of celebrating conversions that God had brought about (Acts 15:3-4).

He approved of us understanding that Christ's followers consist of both Jews and Gentiles and that there is no required behavior distinction between the two (Acts 15:7-9).

He approves of solving division when people listen and reason along divinely authoritative lines of evidence.

He approves of eliminating false teaching (Acts 15:24).

Accounts of approved actions enable us to establish with certainty what God prefers. We discover God's preference when we start with divine answers rather than human questions. Start with answers from God's mind. Do not start with questions from within the human mind. Start with the answers from within scripture. Do not start with questions from within circumstances.

Please internalize and realize these pertinent truths. The mind of God (scripture) holds the answers, while the human mind hosts the questions. Therefore, when we delve into the mind of God, we discover answers, but when we delve into the human mind, we only discover questions.

CHAPTER SEVEN

REPARATIONS

REPARATIONS

Reparations – the making of amends for a wrong one has done by paying money to or otherwise helping those who have been wronged.

The first recorded case of reparations for slavery in the United States involved the former slave Belinda Royal's "pension" in 1783. Though no federal reparations bills have been passed, the 1865 Special Field Orders No. 15 ("Forty Acres and a Mule") is the most well-known attempt to help newly freed slaves integrate into society and accumulate wealth. However, President Andrew Johnson reversed that order and returned the land to its previous owners. Ever since then, reparations have been a politically recurring discussion but no reparations. Proponents in favor and against never seem to agree.

Slavery in America was not new. Throughout the world, humans have enslaved other humans. Slavery in America was not the first. For centuries, the Egyptians enslaved the Hebrews, God's chosen people. People on the continent of Africa enslaved the people of God. Noticeably, America imported slaves from the continent that once enslaved others.

God started the human race with Adam, but with Abram, God started the Hebrew race. God promised Abram that He would prosper him through his posterity, *"After these things the word of the Lord came to Abram in a vision, saying, 'Do not fear, Abram, I am a shield to you; Your reward shall be very great.'*
But Abram said, Lord God, what will You give me, since I am childless, and the heir of my house is Eliezer of Damascus? Abram also said, 'Since You have given me no son, one who has been born in my house is my heir. Then behold, the word of the Lord came to him, saying, This man will not be your heir; but one who will come from your own body shall be your heir'" (Genesis 15:1-4). Abram asked for a surety sign that God would deliver as promised, *"But he said, 'Lord God, how may I know that I will possess it?'"* (Genesis 15:8). God authenticated His promise by revealing that Abram's descendants would be enslaved in a foreign land for 400 years and that they would be released with great wealth, *"Then God said to Abram, 'Know for certain that your descendants will be strangers in a land that is not theirs, where they will be enslaved and oppressed for four hundred years. But I will also judge the nation whom they will serve, and afterward they will come out with many possessions'"* (Genesis 15:13-14). In essence, the Hebrews would receive reparations - be economically repaired (rewarded) for their many years of vigorous labor.

God delivered as promised. When the Hebrews left Egypt, they took flocks, herds, gold, silver, and numerous other precious possessions, *"Take both your flocks and your herds, as you have said, and go, ... for they had requested from the Egyptians articles of silver and articles of gold, and clothing; and the Lord had given the people favor in the sight of the Egyptians, so that they let them have their request. Therefore they plundered the Egyptians"* (Exodus 12:32 &35b-36). According to the favor of God, the Egyptians rewarded the Hebrews.

Because of the fear caused by the Passover plague, and the death of the firstborn of those who were not protected by the blood of the lamb, the Egyptians were almost paying the Hebrews to leave. Thus, they honored the Hebrews' request for materials (Exodus 12:36-38). God certainly knows how to make former slave owners favor former slaves. Later, God would decree that when slaves were set free, they were not to be set free empty-handed, *"If your fellow countryman, a Hebrew man or woman, is sold to you, then he shall serve you for six years, but in the seventh year you shall set him free. And when you set him free, you shall not send him away empty-handed. You shall give generously to him from your flock, your threshing floor, and from your wine vat; you shall give to him as the Lord your*

God has blessed you. And you are to remember that you were a slave in the land of Egypt, and the Lord your God redeemed you; therefore I am commanding this of you today" (Deuteronomy 15:12-15). Yes, the Hebrews left the ghetto with the gold.

As they were releasing them, the Egyptian slaveholders transferred so much wealth to their slaves that when Moses needed resources to build the Tabernacle, there were more than enough. The wealth of the Hebrews enabled them to be unbelievably generous with their Tabernacle contribution. They gave so much they had to be restrained from giving, "*and they said to Moses, 'The people are bringing much more than enough for the construction work which the Lord commanded us to perform.' So Moses issued a command, and circulated a proclamation throughout the camp, saying, 'No man or woman is to perform work any longer for the contributions of the sanctuary.' So the people were restrained from bringing any more. For the material they had was sufficient and more than enough for all the work to perform it*" (Exodus 36:5-7).

Metal Reparations

For some time now, social justice advocates have issued a clarion call for reparations from America for its indulgence in slavery. Reparations are supposed to repair, aren't they? But do they really repair?

Let's examine the lives of the former Hebrew enslaved people and assess the impact reparations (rewards) had on them. For 400 years, the Egyptians held the Hebrews hostage as slaves. After the Passover plague, they released the Hebrews to their freedom (Exodus 12:1-51). When the Hebrews left Egypt, they carried with them an abundance of economic resources, "*Now the sons of Israel had done according to the word of Moses, for they had requested from the Egyptians articles of silver and articles of gold, and clothing; and the Lord had given the people favor in the sight of the Egyptians, so that they let them have their request. Therefore, they plundered the Egyptians*" (Exodus 12:35-36). Now, some scholars say this was a reward rather than reparations. But in any case, they had the metal (silver and gold), whether reparations or rewards, in their possession after many years of forced servitude.

The formerly enslaved people had crossed the Sea and committed themselves to the Lord and Moses' leadership, *"When Israel saw the great power which the Lord had used against the Egyptians, the people feared the Lord, and they believed in the Lord and in His servant Moses"* (Exodus 14:31). Jubilantly, they sang a victory song, exulting the power of God and their release from oppression (Exodus 15:1-21).

In the first month of their deliverance, they wandered into thirst. At Marah, they grumbled against their leader Moses, *"So the people grumbled at Moses, saying, 'What shall we drink?'"* (Exodus 15:24).

In the second month of their deliverance, again, they grumbled, this time about their diet. Threatening Moses, they claimed Moses had brought them into the wilderness to die of starvation. They declared they had a much better life in Egypt and would have preferred to have died in Egypt at God's hand rather than in the wilderness at Moses's hand (Exodus 16:1-3).

A short time later, they are again quarreling with Moses about water. Once again, they asked, *"'Why is it that you have you brought us up from Egypt to kill us and our children and our livestock with thirst?'"* (Exodus 17:3). Wondering out loud, they tested the Lord as if He was no longer among them (Exodus 17:7).

Numerous disputes arose among the Hebrews. Settling their disputes consumed Moses' daily schedule (Exodus 18:13-26). Their conflicts were so burdensome that they almost wore Moses out.

Can you believe this? They had begun to enslave each other. Yes, the formerly enslaved people had begun buying and selling each other (Exodus 21:1-11). How sad and how far they had sunk to begin engaging in the slave trade?

As if this was not enough, they began suffocating the life out of their kin. Even premeditated murder ran rampant. Not only were they killing their neighbors, but they had begun to murder their parents (Exodus 21:12-15).

Their list of atrocities sounds like the local newspaper of any major US city. Debauchery everywhere was taking place: kidnapping, cursing parents, allowing wayward animals to sore people to death, stealing livestock, sexual sins, sorcery, bestiality, elderly abuse, child abuse, loan sharking, etc. (Exodus 21:12-22:31).

Unfortunately, their moral climate continually declined. God warned them to be faithful to His commands. Despite this, they persisted in faithless rebellion. Therefore, God led the initial generation that crossed the Sea to die in the wilderness, *"So the Lord said, 'I have forgiven them in accordance with your word; however, as I live, all the earth will be filled with the glory of the Lord. Certainly all the people who have seen My glory and My signs which I performed in Egypt and in the wilderness, yet have put Me to the test these ten times and have not listened to My voice, shall by no means see the land which I swore to their fathers, nor shall any of those who were disrespectful to Me see it'"* (Numbers 14:20-23).

They were free from Egyptian supremacy and had received metal reparations. Were they repaired and made whole? Is this grumbling about food, consistent quarreling about water, daily disputing among each other, operating a slave market of their fellow Hebrews, murdering their parents, etc., consistent with repaired people? Absolutely not!

Metal reparations did minimal, if anything, to repair them. Likely among them, their freedom allowed them to commit more crimes than did their slavery. Apparently, metal reparations do not improve relations between man and man. Therefore, I conclude that only reparations between God and man repair the relationship between man and man, *"For He Himself is our peace, who made both groups into one and broke down the barrier of the dividing wall, by abolishing in His flesh the hostility, which is the Law composed of commandments expressed in ordinances, so that in Himself He might make the two one new person, in this way establishing peace; and that He might reconcile them both in one body to God through the cross, by it having put to death the hostility"* (Ephesians 2:14-16).

Mental Reparations

God chose Abram and created the Hebrew race through him. Later, God would change his name to Abraham. He promised to bless not only Abram but all the families of the Earth (Genesis 12:1-3). So how did Abram's descendants, the Hebrews, end up in Egypt in slavery?

Famine paved the road to slavery. A famine came about during the lifetime of Abram. He sought refuge in Egypt, *"Now there was a famine in the land; so Abram went down to Egypt to live there for a time, because the famine was severe in the land"* (Genesis 12:10). Another famine came during the lifetime of Isaac, Abraham's son. This time, God cautioned him not to enter Egypt (Genesis 26:1-3). Yet again, another famine occurred during the lifetime of Jacob, Abraham's grandson (Genesis 42:1-2). Jacob sent his sons to Egypt to buy grain. This time, Egypt rescued the Hebrews from the famine but subsequently reduced them to slaves.

Now, let's digress. When Jacob's son, Joseph, was just a child, his brothers hated him (Genesis 37:3-4). Their hatred erupted into a murderous plot to destroy him and his dreams (Genesis 37:18-20). Fortunately, the God of favor aborted that plan. Instead, Joseph's brothers sold him to a band of Ishmaelites (Genesis 37:28). The Ishmaelites sold him to Potiphar's, the captain of Pharaoh's bodyguard (Genesis 39:1). This sale stripped the 17-year-old child, Joseph, of his family, culture, and language and took him more than 500 miles away into Egyptian slavery.

A traumatic experience impacted the teenage mind of Joseph. Surely, Joseph will, if ever released, suffer from post-traumatic slave syndrome. Won't he? Let's see.

Joseph successfully served as a slave. Because he served with dedicated discipline, Potiphar promoted him and placed his own household under Joseph's jurisdiction (Genesis 39:4). However, this was to be short-lived. Potiphar's wife developed a sensuous attraction for Joseph. When he spurned her request, she lied to her husband, resulting in Joseph being imprisoned.

It was awful enough to be a slave in a foreign land, but now Joseph was a slave in prison in a foreign land (Genesis 39:19-20). But Joseph continued to dedicate himself to the task and discipline himself. Therefore, God favored him, and Potiphar promoted him in prison. Due to God's favor again, Pharaoh promoted him out of prison (Genesis 39:22, 41:39-49).

Throughout his life, Joseph recognized the presence and power of God, *"But Joseph said to them, 'Do not be afraid, for am I in God's place? As for you, you meant evil against me, but God meant it for good in order to bring about this present result, to keep many people alive'"* (Genesis 50:19-20). Joseph endured slavery and suffered not from post-traumatic slave syndrome. He was not guilty of mismanagement, misuse, and abuse of his kin or anyone else. His post-slavery behavior would be quite unlike his ancestors years later when they were released from slavery.

His ancestors, the Hebrews, received metal (gold and silver) reparations, yet their behavior toward each other continually declined. They sank so low that God gave them up into slavery again. Because of their idolatry, the 10 Northern tribes, Israel fell into the hands of the Assyrians, *"Now in the fourth year of King Hezekiah, which was the seventh year of Hoshea son of Elah King of Israel, Shalmaneser king of Assyria marched against Samaria and besieged it. And at the end of three years they captured it; in the sixth year of Hezekiah, which was the ninth year of Hoshea King of Israel, Samaria was captured. Then the king of Assyria led Israel into exile to Assyria, and put them in Halah and on the Habor, the river of Gozan, and in the cities of the Medes. This happened because they did not obey the voice of the Lord their God, but violated His covenant, all that Moses the servant of the Lord had commanded; they would neither listen nor do it"* (2 Kings 18:9-12).

Later, because of their idolatry, the two southern tribes, Judah, fell into the hands of the Babylonians, *"And the Lord sent against him bands of Chaldeans, bands of Arameans, bands of Moabites, and bands of Ammonites. He sent them against Judah to destroy it, in accordance with the word of the Lord which He had spoken through His servants the prophets. It indeed came upon Judah at the command of the Lord, to remove them from His sight due to the sins of Manasseh, in accordance with everything that he had done, and also for the innocent blood which he shed, for he filled Jerusalem with innocent blood; and the Lord was unwilling to forgive. Now the rest of the acts of Jehoiakim and all that he did, are they not written in the Book of the Chronicles of the Kings of Judah"* (2 Kings 24:2-5). They lived quite unlike their forefather, Joseph. How sad it is for a family legacy to deteriorate.

Metal reparations will not help when mental reparations are needed. Mental reparations are needed not because of what operates in the heart of the captor but because of what is *not* operating in the heart of the captured. Spiritual stamina enables the captured to be fully repaired by God, not his captor.

What repaired Joseph? Not metals! But a better question is not what repaired Joseph but Who repaired him? God was with Joseph (Genesis 39:2-3, 21, 23). How was God with him? In Joseph's mind and heart, God was with him. In his mind and heart, Joseph knew that God was with Him. The only indicator that God was with him was in Joseph's mind and heart when he was in the pit. When Joseph was in prison, the only indicator that God was with him was in his mind and heart. Joseph was physically enslaved, yet his mind and heart remained free.

Free your mind before freeing your body. Before metal reparations, slaves needed mental reparations. They, not their oppressor, must release their mind and heart from bondage. Otherwise, they will do to others what others have done to them. Now you understand why the Hebrews began to enslave their fellow countrymen. Now you understand why criminals run rampant, claiming their behavior is the inherent vestige of slavery. In some categories, the formerly-called "Negro" often behaves worse 150 years after slavery than he did 150 months after slavery. Entertainment, sports, and social media, not slavery, continue to corrupt minds and hearts. But it does not have to be. We can renew our minds (Ephesians 4:20-24).

Joseph was enslaved, yet he did not need metal repair. He was hated by his brothers and sold at age 17. Why did he not need repair? He was never ruined! His focus sustained him. It's one thing to be enslaved with your group, but to be enslaved alone and stripped of culture and language is far more grave. He never let his mind become corrupted. Now that so many of us have corrupted our minds, we must renew our minds. How?

God designed the human being as a spirit, soul, and body system. Within the system of the human soul, He designed three faculties: the intellect (mind), intent (will), and intensity (emotions). Through the Roman letter, God pleaded for renewing the human mind, the intellect (Romans 12:1-2).

Only when we follow divine counsel do we enjoy the maximum quality of health of the human mind. Divine counsel calls for a renewing of the mind. What is the design of the human mind, the intellect?

The mind consists of a conscious component. Our conscious mind receives, reviews, and retains *a small portion of the data* that appears to us. Our conscious mind consists of our recallable memory.

The mind consists of a subconscious component. Our subconscious mind receives, reviews, and retains *all the data* that appears to us. Our subconscious mind consists of our recallable and suppressed memory [hypnosis].

The mind consists of a conscience component. Our conscience mind receives, reviews, and retains *the data assigned moral and/or ethical value*. Our conscience mind consists of our belief system, the product of accepted teachings.

Divine counsel calls for a renewing of the mind. To fully renew the mind, we must condition and culture it at the conscious and subconscious levels (Matthew 22:41); (Matthew 26:73-73). Unintentionally and unaware, we do absorb from our environment. Therefore, we need to guard our minds within our environment. In addition to conditioning and culturing our minds at the conscious and subconscious levels, we must also condition and culture our minds at the conscience level. Yes, we must intellectually and intentionally assign moral and ethical value according to God's word (Romans 12:2). We must have a will (intent) to honor all the conditioning and culturing of our mind and add intensity (emotion) to our will to honor the conditioning and culturing of your mind.

God wants you to intensify how you honor your conscience mind. Select one moral or ethical value and write a note to a friend telling them how you will intensify your honoring of that one value.

Conclusion

Metal reparations without mental reparations will be useless. The oppressor cannot repair the mind of the oppressed. Real repair is between the slave and God. Remember, righteousness, not economics, exalts the nation (Proverbs 14:34). Nothing short of mental reparations will repair any human being, whether slave or free, *"But you did not learn Christ in this way, if indeed you have heard Him and have been taught in Him, just as truth is in Jesus, that, in reference to your former way of life, you are to rid yourselves of the old self, which is being corrupted in accordance with the lusts of deceit, and that you are to be renewed in the spirit of your minds, and to put on the new self, which in the likeness of God has been created in righteousness and holiness of the truth"* (Ephesians 4:20-24).

God is the source of all blessings; He possesses the power to give us all we need. The earlier scriptures document this in 1 Chronicles 29:11-12, 14, 26-28, 25, while the later scriptures document this in 1 Corinthians 4:7. Acknowledging the source of blessings enables us to improve our prosperity.

What is your view of God? Where did you obtain it? Do you see God as a the One who desires not only for His people to prosper but for the world to see their prosperity? If not, why not? It's time, break the poverty cycle!

8
CHAPTER EIGHT

FOR THE RECORD

FOR THE RECORD

BECOME SAVED – The Basis of Salvation
The first mention of blood was Abel's (Genesis 4:10). The last mention of blood was Jesus' (Revelation 19:13). In between times, God sprinkled blood around, about, and all upon His people (Exodus 24:6-8, 29:15-21).

Scripture reveals that the blood of Christ cleanses us from the guilt of sin as we are born into the family of God (1 Peter 1:17-19; Revelation 1:4-6). Grace made the cleansing power of the blood available, but faith activates it (Exodus 12-14; 1 Corinthians 10:1-4).

Scripture reveals that the blood of Christ cleanses us from the guilt of sin after we are born into the family of God (1 John 1:5-2:1; Ephesians 1:3-8). Forgiveness is durative even for those who are not living a perfectly sinless life.

God wants you to think thoroughly about the blood of Jesus. Never ask, "Can God forgive the sinner?" On the basis of the blood of Jesus, God can forgive sinners. Never ask, "Will God forgive the saint?" On the basis of the blood of Jesus, God will forgive saints. God wants you to celebrate the power of the blood (Exodus 12:13, 1 Corinthians 10:1-4; John 19:34). God is a bloody God. The bible is a bloody book. Believers, God's people, are a bloody people.

Moses negotiated with Pharaoh for the release of the Israelites from captivity. Only after the Passover, the tenth plague, did Pharaoh release the Israelites. But, as they traveled toward the Promised Land, Pharaoh changed his mind and pursued after them.

With his army, Pharaoh sandwiched the Israelites against the Red Sea (Exodus 14:5-9). God provided salvation (Exodus 14:13-14). Salvation was a military term describing an escape from a position of danger to a position of safety.

Salvation is a deliverance from an old relationship. In their old relationship, they served Pharaoh (Exodus 1:8-14; 5:1-14). In our old relationship, we served sin (John 8:34, Romans 6:16-17). Actively, we do that which the Lord does not authorize (1 John 3:4). Passively, we refuse to do that which the Lord does authorize (James 4:17; Luke 12:47-48).

Salvation is a deliverance from an old relationship to a new relationship. In their new relationship, they served Moses. In our new relationship, we serve righteousness (Romans 6:16-18). Actively, we do that which the Lord authorizes. Passively, we refuse to do that which the Lord does not authorize.
Of the several types of salvation the Bible speaks of, the relationships delivered from and to may differ; however, the principle of the process of the deliverance remains the same. Salvation takes place according to an authorized process.

- A) For their salvation from Pharaoh:
    1) The Lord, who provided salvation, responded.
    2) The Lord's spokesperson, who informed them of the salvation, responded.
    3) The endangered people, who needed to receive the salvation, responded.

God provided this salvation for them and Paul called it a baptism (1 Corinthians 10:1-2). This process was: (a) necessary, (b) different, (c) humanly illogical, but (d) successful.
  A) For our salvation from sin:
    1) The Lord, who provides salvation, has responded. He sent Jesus as your sin substitute.
    2) The Lord's spokesperson, informs you of salvation.
    3) The endangered people, you, who need to receive this salvation, need to respond.

Salvation from sin is a deliverance from an old relationship to a new relationship by way of an authorized process. This process was: (a) necessary, (b) different, (c) humanly illogical, but (d) successful. Salvation is not a biological, economical, or racial issue, but a scriptural issue (2 Timothy 3:15).

The blood was shed (Exodus 12:1-28). Yet, Israel had not been freed from their slavery to Egypt. Why? There was something they needed to do. They had to go through the waters of baptism (Exodus 14:21-25, 1 Corinthians 10:1-2).

The blood of Jesus has been made available. Unfortunately, all are not saved. Why? Reconciliation was accomplished at the cross but is appropriated at conversion (baptism). Those who are unsaved have not come to enjoy the appropriation of the blood of Jesus. For example: The college student's school loan for the year is accomplished when the university approves it, but the loan is appropriated at the beginning of each semester when the student registers. Your earnings are accomplished each hour, but appropriated when you receive the paycheck.

Many are unsaved because they have no faith response to the resurrection of Jesus. Salvation is accomplished for them, but not yet appropriated to them. Salvation will be appropriated to them when they engage in the behavior (baptism) that leads to salvation.

First Implementation of God's Plan of Salvation (Acts 2)
The law of "first mention" may be said to be the principle that requires you to go to that portion of the Scripture where a doctrine is mentioned for the first time and to study the first occurrence of the same in order to get the fundamental inherent meaning of that doctrine. When you thus see the first appearance, which is usually in the simplest form, you can then examine the doctrine in other portions of the Word that were given later. You shall see that the fundamental concept in the first occurrence remains dominant as a rule and directs (interprets) all later additions to that doctrine.

HEAR THE GOSPEL - In order for you to be saved, you must hear the gospel. The gospel is the good news of the availability of the salvation that has been provided for by the grace of God and the sacrificial blood of Jesus. The death, burial, and the resurrection of Jesus are the certified facts of the gospel (1 Corinthians 15:1-4). Hearing the gospel is one of the certified obedience requirements of the gospel.

Acts 2:1-4: The apostles preached a Holy Spirit-directed sermon. This was the first sermon preached to unsaved people after the resurrection of Jesus. Therefore, we can apply the "law of first mention".

Acts 2:6-8: In their own (native) language, the people heard the Holy Spirit-directed sermon.

Acts 2:29-33: The people heard the certified facts (death, burial, resurrection) of the gospel of Jesus Christ.

Acts 2:36-37: Hearing the fact of the resurrection of Jesus, the Man they had crucified, pierced their heart. Yes, this sermon irritated their conscience.

BELIEVE THE GOSPEL - In order for you to be saved, you must believe the gospel. To believe the gospel is to intellectually and emotionally embrace the facts of the death, burial, and resurrection of Jesus.

Acts 2:12-16: Though they understood verbally what was said, at first some did not know the meaning of the message experience. Therefore, they asked, "…What does this mean?" Some of the people suggested that the apostles were experiencing drunkenness. Therefore, they said, "…They are full of sweet wine."

Acts 2:22-24: Though they did not initially know the meaning of this message, when they were reminded of the ministry of Jesus, they could not help but believe their knowledge of what God had done through Jesus.

Acts 2:32-33: God had raised Jesus from the dead and exalted Him. Again, they were reminded of what they had already observed "…we are all witnesses. … this which you both see and hear."

Acts 2:37: Because they believed that God had raised up to life the very Man they had put down to death, the preached word pierced their heart, and irritated their conscience.

Acts 2:41: Because they had come to believe that Jesus was the Son of God, they received the word.

REPENT OF SIN - In order for you to be saved, you must repent. Repentance is your change of heart that takes place in your mind (Matthew 21:28-32). In repentance, you change your allegiance (Acts 17:30, 26:19-20). Repentance is a resetting of your allegiance. It is a resetting of your allegiance from your selfish self to the Savior.

Acts 2:38: The Holy Spirit led the apostle Peter to command the people to repent of having opposed God, "Peter said to them, repent…"

Acts 2:41-42: Earlier, they rejected the word and crucified Jesus. But now, they are receiving the word and embracing Jesus as the Son of God. This change of heart indicates their repentance.

CONFESS THAT JESUS IS THE SON OF GOD - In order for you to be saved, you must confess. What does it mean to confess? Confess is translated from a compound word (homlogeo) that means to speak the same. Therefore, to confess is to admit (John 1:20, 12:42). To confess is to acknowledge (Romans 10:9, 14:10-12, Hebrews 13:15). Confess means that you agree at heart and speak the same thing as another (1 John 1:10).

Acts 2:37: God said that Jesus is His Son (Matthew 3:16-17). Therefore, the people must admit that Jesus was the Son of God. By asking, "what shall we do", they admitted that they had come to believe the gospel that had been preached. Yes, they agreed with and acknowledged the truth of the fact that Jesus was the Son of God.

BECOME BAPTIZED – In order for you to be saved, you must be baptized. Baptism is your faith response of being buried in water in response to the fact that Jesus Christ is the Son of God (Acts 8:12; 37-39; 1 Peter 3:21). Baptism is mentioned some 92 times in the New Testament. Interestingly, Jesus began His earthly ministry being baptized of John in the Jordan River (Matthew 3:13-17) and concluded His ministry by commanding His apostles to baptize those who would become His disciples (Matthew 28:19-20). **Obviously, baptism is essential.**

Acts 2:38: The Holy Spirit led the apostle Peter to command them to *"... be baptized in the name of Jesus Christ for the forgiveness of our sins..."* The purpose for which they were to become baptized harmonized with the earlier statement of Jesus (Mark 16:16). This was the first time the apostles had ever taught about baptism. This was the first time the apostles had ever told a person to become baptized. Though Jesus had taught the relationship between baptism and salvation, this was the first time the apostles had ever taught the inherent relationship between baptism and salvation. The "law of first mention" must be considered in this instance.

Acts 2:40-42: Obviously, those in the audience believed that there existed an inherent relationship between baptism and salvation, for 3,000 people who received His word were baptized that same day.

BECOME SAVED – The Relationship Between Baptism and Salvation

Read: Mark 16:16
Where did Jesus place baptism; before salvation or after salvation?

Why is there so much confusion on the subject of baptism? An intellectual "exegesis" [reading out of] of scripture rather than an emotional "eisegesis" [reading into] of scripture peels away most of the layers of confusion. Let's proceed.

The Holy Spirit could not come until after Jesus had risen from the dead and ascended to heaven (John 16:7). Some 40 days after Jesus had risen from the dead, the Holy Spirit was yet to come (Acts 1:1-8). The Holy Spirit came on the day of Pentecost (Acts 2:1-4).

The Holy Spirit revealed the message of truth to those who wrote scripture (Ephesians 3:1-5, 2 Peter 1:21). The apostle Peter spoke the words of Acts 2:38 before Matthew, Mark, Luke, and John wrote the words contained in their Gospels. Being from regions beyond Jerusalem, most of those who heard the words of Acts 2:38 had not heard Jesus speak (Acts 2:9-11). Even those who had heard Jesus speak had failed to understand His message; therefore, they crucified Him (John 20:30, Acts 3:29).

Historically, the Jews had offered sacrifices with an understanding that they would invoke the forgiveness (appeasement) of God. Even on Pentecost, they believed that they needed to respond in order to receive forgiveness of God. Therefore, they asked, "What shall we do" (Acts 2:37).

Peter had just preached a persuasive sermon designed to convince the audience that Jesus was the Christ and Lord (Acts 2:36). Obviously, some who heard, also believed, for their hearts were pricked (Acts 2:37). Hearts are never pricked until belief comes. In addition to believing, they asked what to do. In other words, they were now asking, "After believing what (else) shall we do? If they had been forgiven [saved] just by believing, then Peter should have told them so. Otherwise, he accommodated their false belief about doing something, in addition to believing in order to be saved.

In the past, they had killed and offered an animal in their effort to receive forgiveness of sins. Peter informed them that no longer would they have to kill a lamb. The Lamb (Jesus) had already been slain. They must now repent and be baptized to embrace the death of Jesus.
Only after Jesus had been raised from the dead did He teach of the cause and effect relationship of baptism with salvation.

But what about Romans 10:9-10? Let's set the stage.

> 1. Those to whom the apostle Paul addressed this letter were called and had become saints (see Romans 1:6-7).
>
> 2. They had died to sin (see Romans 6:2).
>
> 3. They had been baptized into Christ and His death (see Romans 6:3).
>
> 4. They had been raised from the dead to walk in the newness of life (see Romans 6:4).
>
> 5. They had become united with Jesus (see Romans 6:5).
>
> 6. Their old self had been crucified with Christ (see Romans 6:6).
>
> 7. They had obeyed from the heart the doctrinal teachings (see Romans 6:17).
>
> 8. They had been freed from sin (see Romans 6:18).
>
> 9. They had become servants of righteousness (see Romans 6:18).

Believers from Rome had been at Pentecost and likely had been baptized then (Acts 2:10). Hence, the apostle Paul said to the believers, those who had already been baptized "confess and believe" (Romans 10:9-10).

Many people have read or heard this, *"for by grace you have been saved through faith"* and concluded that grace and faith excludes baptism (Ephesians 2:8). It is true that the apostle wrote this statement about the believers of Ephesus. What can we definitely know from scripture that will shed light on the subject? Let's look further.

Had not the Ephesians, those in Ephesus, heard the message of truth (Ephesians 1:13)? Had not the Ephesians, those in Ephesus, believed the message of truth?

Had not the Ephesians, those in Ephesus, been baptized? Acts 19:1-5
Those believers to whom the apostle Paul wrote, had heard the gospel, believed the gospel, and had been baptized. The grace and faith that saved them included baptism.

BECOME SAVED – Holy Spirit-led Post Resurrection Understanding of Baptism

Most of the biblical information about baptism comes after Jesus had been resurrected from the dead. The Holy Spirit guided the apostles and prophets as they spoke and wrote about baptism. Through the Holy Spirit, God provided a more comprehensive understanding of the role and relationship of baptism.

Read: Acts 8:26-40
The eunuch did not understand what he was reading from Isaiah 53:7ff (Acts 8:30-32). Philip began at Isaiah 53:7, the place where the eunuch was reading, and preached unto him Jesus (Acts 8:35).

How could Philip preach Jesus when the name Jesus is not once stated in Isaiah 53?

How could Philip demand that the eunuch believe that Jesus Christ is the Son of God when believing that Jesus Christ is the Son of God is never stated in Isaiah 53?

How could Philip introduce the subject of baptism while preaching Jesus from Isaiah 53 when baptism is not stated in Isaiah 53?
How could Philip understand Isaiah 53 when the eunuch did not?
The answers to all four questions are the same. Philip had a Holy Spirit-led post-resurrection understanding of the Old Testament scripture (Acts 6:5) and the eunuch did not.

God had more fully revealed His will to the apostles and prophets (Ephesians 3:5). There are some things that had not been understood before, but came to be understood only after the resurrection of Jesus and the coming enlightening provided through the Holy Spirit. Because Philip had a Holy Spirit-led post-resurrection understanding of the Old Testament scripture, God enlightened him to understand things more fully than did others. God enlightened His apostles and prophets to understand the Old Testament. When we read the New Testament, we gain insight into the inspired minds of the apostles and prophets (Ephesians 3:5).

Jesus recognized that men needed a post-resurrection understanding of the Old Testament scripture. Therefore, He opened their minds to understand the scriptures (Luke 24:44-47).

God opened Lydia's mind to understand (Acts 16:14). Her understanding led to her being baptized (Acts 16:15).

Where does Old Testament teach the purpose of baptism? It does not; it just illustrates it. The lamb's blood became available for the Israelites (Exodus 12:21-28). Yet, the Israelites were not free from bondage until they passed through the sea (Exodus 14:26-29). God saved Israel on the day that they passed through the water (Exodus 14:30). The Holy Spirit's inspired commentary called that experience a baptism, *"For I do not want you to be unaware, brethren, that our fathers were all under the cloud and all passed through the sea; and all were baptized into Moses in the cloud and in the sea; and all ate the same spiritual food; and all drank the same spiritual drink, for they were drinking from a spiritual rock which followed them; and the rock was Christ"* (1 Corinthians 10:1-4).

BECOME SAVED – The Dry Side of Baptism

Read: Matthew 28:18-20
When did Jesus teach about baptism, before or after salvation?

Read: Mark 16:15-18
What did Jesus say were the prerequisites of salvation?

Read: Acts 2:38
What did the apostle Peter say was the purpose of baptism?

To His apostles, Jesus made a few final remarks after His resurrection. Baptism was one of the topics that He discussed with them (Matthew 28:18-20; Mark 16:15-18). Clearly, the baptism of new believers is of vital significance to the Lord Jesus. God-fearing believers want to know that Christ approves of their baptism. Our baptism indicates that the reality of our death with Christ is a realized fact. Our baptism indicates that the reality of our death with Christ is a ruling force. Near the beginning of his ministry, the apostle Peter preached about baptism (Acts 2:38). Near the ending of his ministry, the apostle Peter wrote about baptism.

Read: 1 Peter 3:21
What does this text say that baptism does?

Ineed, the apostle Peter reminded the believers of the importance of baptism. First, we consider the "dry" side of baptism. It is a response of the mind; for it is an internal appeal toward God. The dry side is a response of the conscience. The conscience is a product of accepted teachings (John 8:1-9; Leviticus 20:10). If you have been taught to be honest and you accept that as valid, whenever you are dishonest you violate your conscience. Your conscience then causes you to feel guilty. On the other hand, if you were taught to be honest and you consider that invalid, then you do not violate your conscience. Therefore, you feel no guilt.

The dry side is a response of a ***good conscience.*** Within this context, a good conscience is a heart that trusts in the resurrection of Jesus Christ (1 Peter 3: 21). The resurrection proves that Jesus is the Son of God (Romans 1:4; Acts 17:31). Only those who believe in the resurrection of Jesus have a good conscience for baptism (John 8:24; Acts 8:35-37).

If one's conscience is insufficiently taught, then it will be insufficiently developed. And if one's conscience is incorrectly taught, then it will be incorrectly developed. A good conscience results from having accepted wholesome teachings. When taught insufficiently, conscience insufficiently develops (Acts 19:1-5). When taught erroneously, then conscience erroneously develops.

The Israelites, after seeing the power of God displayed through him, were baptized into Moses as their deliverer (Exodus 14:31; 1 Corinthians 10:2). We, after hearing about the power of God displayed through the resurrection of Jesus, (Romans 1:1-4) are then baptized into Christ as our Savior. To identify with Jesus and rely on Him for salvation from sin, we must be baptized.

What really happens at baptism?

John the Baptist announced that he baptized in water, but that Jesus would baptize with the Holy Spirit (Matthew 3:11; Mark. 1:8; Luke. 3:16; John 1:33). He made this statement to the general population before Jesus ever began choosing His apostles. What did he mean?

By the Holy Spirit, Jesus baptizes us all into the one body of Christ (1 Corinthians 12:13). Persons whom Jesus baptizes by the Holy Spirit are all truly members of His one body, without regard to earthly distinctions (1 Corinthians 12:13; Galatians 3:2627; Ephesians 2:18). The baptism work of the Holy Spirit has to do with the body of Christ, the church. By the Spirit baptism we are immersed into the body of Christ. Here, the Spirit is the instrument, the agent who places the believer into the body of Christ. The creation of the one body is the result of the baptism work of the Holy Spirit. At the moment of salvation, the baptism work of the Holy Spirit inducts the believer as a living member into the body of Christ.

They, who are baptized by the Holy Spirit, may continue to draw refreshment and spiritual nourishment from that same inexhaustible source (John 4:1314; John 7:3739). Speaking in tongues is not the indispensable sign of the baptism work of the Holy Spirit. In the first century, even as now, every Christian experienced the baptism work of the Holy Spirit. Not even then in the first century did every Christian speak in tongues (1 Corinthians 12:30).

BECOME SAVED – The Wet Side of Baptism

Secondly, we consider the "wet" side of baptism. The wet side is a response of the body; for it is an external appeal towards God. The wet side consists of a **burial in water.**

The word "covenant" is of Latin origin. It is derived from the two words "com" = together and "venire" = to come. It meant a literal coming together.

The corresponding Hebrew word for covenant meant "to cut, to eat" as in the cutting asunder of the victims which were sacrificed at the making of a covenant (Genesis 15:9-21; Jeremiah 34:18-19). To eat, probably referred to the eating of the slain victims. To eat with someone was commonly regarded as almost equivalent to making a covenant with that person (Genesis 31:43-55; Exodus 24:1-2, 9-11).

Offering sacrifices also ratified covenants (Genesis 15:7-21; Exodus 24:3-8; Jeremiah 34:17-22). It was accepted that the sacrificial blood has the sacramental power to bind together two parties in a covenant (1 Corinthians 11:25). The Greeks had two words that conveyed the concept of covenant:
(1) *suntheke* - devoted solemn agreement made between equals
(2) *diatheke* - agreement made by superior for the acceptance and observing of an inferior

All of God's covenants are *diatheke*. A covenant must include three items: (1) covenantor, (2) covenantee, and (3) various stipulations of the contract. A covenant was a firm confirmed commitment (Hebrews 6:13-17).

Through Abram, God teaches us that commitment comes by covenant. Within each covenant there exists the core essence of the covenant and a ceremonial expression of the covenant.

God promised Abram that He would bless all the earth through him and his descendants (Genesis 12:3-5). God revealed the core essence of His covenant with Abram (Genesis 17:16; 19). He then required Abram to participate in the ceremonial expression of His covenant. Participation in the ceremonial expression of the covenant is essential to the strengthening of faith in the core essence of the covenant.

How would God have responded to Abraham if he neglected to participate in the ceremony of the covenant?

There is the ceremonial expression (ceremony) of the name change (Genesis 17:3-8; 15). God required Abram to change his and Sarai's name. There is the ceremonial expression of circumcision (Genesis 17:10-14; 23-27). God required Abraham to circumcise himself, his son and his male servants. Participation in the ceremonial expression of the covenant is essential to strengthening faith in the core essence of the covenant. Therefore, the core of the covenant is inherently attached to the ceremonial expression of the covenant. Abraham had to participate in ceremonial expression of the covenant in order to enjoy the core essence of the covenant. He could not bypass the name change and the circumcision and expect to enjoy the blessing of the covenant.

We cannot separate the two. We should not seek to separate thinking about the Lord's Supper from eating the elements (1 Corinthians 11:23-28). We cannot separate immersion from baptism (1 Peter 3:21). We cannot think the Lord's Supper into existence. We must participate in it. We cannot think baptism into existence. We must participate in it. A failure to participate in the ceremonial expression indicates ignorance or absence of integrity. The ceremonial expression of the covenant is inherently attached to the core essence of the covenant.

The term "baptism" never means sprinkle or pour, but to immerse (Acts 8:38-39; John 3:23; Matthew 27:57-60). It is not only important that baptism is practiced, but how it is practiced. It is a picture of our death, burial, and resurrection with Jesus (Romans 6:1-4). Baptism is an immersion. The fact of the definition and the fact of the illustration assure that (Acts 8:38-39). The wet side consists of a burial in water in order **to receive the benefits of the resurrection of Jesus** (1 Peter 3:21). Only when an immersion takes place for this purpose, is it valid (Acts 19:3-5).

God used the waters of the flood to save eight people during the days of Noah (1 Peter 3:20). What happens now? God uses the waters of baptism to save all who trust in the resurrection of Jesus Christ (1 Peter 3:21). The symbol preceded the real essence (Romans 5:14; Hebrews 9:24). The waters of the flood were a figure or type of baptism. Obviously, baptism consisted of that which one might think to be an external cleansing. Only if water was used, one might mistake baptism to be an external cleansing.

If you have experienced only the dry side, then you have only experienced half of a baptism. Half of a baptism is no baptism at all. You need to be immersed today. If you experienced only the wet side then there is no baptism at all. You need to be immersed today. The dry side must precede the wet side, and the wet side must follow the dry side for it to be a valid baptism. Baptism stands between you and salvation. God calls you to be baptized today.

BECOME DEVOTED – In order for a person to maximize the experience of salvation, he/she must become devoted to the instructions of the apostles. Now that you have been baptized into the body of Christ, you must learn to participate in kingdom practices so as to enjoy kingdom privileges. Always honor your kingdom citizenship.

Acts 2:41-42: On the day of Pentecost about 3,000 listeners received the word. To receive the word is to welcome the word (Luke 8:40). Those disciples who received and welcomed the word continually devoted themselves (remained faithfully in place, Acts 1:14, 2:46, 6:4, 8:13, 10:7).

They continually devoted themselves to the apostles' teachings [(doctrine, tutoring) Acts 2:42; Titus 1:9]. Teachings from the apostles originated with God (Acts 2:4; John 14:26, 7:16). Apostolic teachings were not stagnant, but were living principles that changed behavior and revolutionized the world.

They continually devoted themselves to fellowship (Acts 2:42). Through fellowship, they pledged their allegiance to each other. They expressed allegiance by participating in compatible activity because of their compatible interest (1 John 1:3, 6-7; 2 Corinthians 13:14; Philippians 2:1).

They continually devoted themselves to worship (Acts 2:42-43, 46a, 47). God wants our worship to become a matter of spiritual conviction. For us, worship should become more than just a matter of selfish convenience.

Expand Your Knowledge with These Essential Reads by John Davis Marshall

"Good and Angry" - A Personal Guide to Anger Management

"The Power of the Tongue" – What You Say is What You Get

"God, Listen" – Prayers That God Always Answers [includes a 50-day addiction recovery guide]

"Final Answer"

"Success is a God Idea"

"Show Me the Money" – 7 Exercises That Build Economic Strength.

"God Knows" – There is no Need to Worry.

"My God" – Who He is Will Change Your Life.

"Faith, Family, & Finances" Vol. One –. Essential Truths That Lead to Passionate Happiness.

"Faith, Family, & Finances" Vol. Two - The Mess We are in and How to Get Out of It!

"A Queen In Search of A King" – Go Ahead and Ask Him for a Date!

"Church Matters" – Passionate Pleadings That Prepare Us For The Future

"Hallelujah" – Worship Him According to His Preference

"Called to be a Champion" – Coaching Yourself Into the Champion Circle

"Pre Marriage Preparations" – From Me to We

"Man HANDLE IT"

"Husband Love Your Wife" – Even Though She Does Not Want You To

"Wife be Subject to Your Husband" – Even Though He Does Not Want You To

"Reparations" – Break the Poverty Cycle

"Wisdom" – Things I Should Have Learned When I Was A Teenager But Didn't

www.JohnDavisMarshall.com

www.ingramcontent.com/pod-product-compliance
Lightning Source LLC
LaVergne TN
LVHW010410070526
838199LV00065B/5942